25 Poems for People Who Don't Read Poetry

Selected and with an introduction by the editors of
Abandoned Mine, a poetry journal

Published by *Abandoned Mine*, a poetry journal.

ISBN: 979-8-218-49147-5

For the poets and readers

Additional Books in This Series:

43 Poems for People Who Don't Read Poetry

Contents

Author Bios

Special Thanks

The Key Word is Yet

On our website (abandonedmine.org) and in the introduction to our first anthology (*43 Poems for People Who Don't Read Poetry*), we articulate the reasons why we started *Abandoned Mine*, reasons we won't repeat here—save for the opening sentence:

We started this journal—we published this book—for people who don't yet read poetry.

The key word in that sentence is *yet*.

We believe that most people have a hunger for soul-stirring. A hunger for emotional and spiritual growth. A hunger to see more clearly. A hunger for connection. A hunger to be seen.

Poetry can feed this hunger.

It's only a matter of time before more people discover (or re-discover) it!

We hope that this book will be part of that discovery, that nourishing.

Warmly,
Jasen Christensen & Robert Grant
Co-editors

A Note on Formatting and Title

Due to this book's dimensions and margins, the following poems appear with line breaks that are different than the line breaks that appear on our website:

- "The Yearbook of the Mind" by Gabriella Brand
- "Amusement" by Craig Cotter
- "Glaucous" by Sara Eddy
- "*Siempre,*" by Sarah Stern

To view these poems as the authors intended them to appear, please read them on our website—on a computer or in the landscape orientation on your phone or tablet.

Also, Prartho Sereno's poem "Practice Run" was first published on our website under the title "Starfall."

Poems

Practicing for the Carnival
Laura Winter

a giraffe
in velvet and feather boas
stilts down the street,
juggles tree branches
along the way.

children stop
their play
and the fireman asks
what are you?

she bends wide
and low,
reaches for
the astonished smallness
of his hand,
what ever you want me to be.

Self-Portrait?

Don Colburn

The emcee for tonight's reading beckons me
out of the coffee line, brandishing her notepad.
Wants me to know that introducing poets
is a waste of time for everyone.
How could I not like Terri, her lack of slack,
her tone so right-on that I take her seriously
even if she's joking. Today her hair is purple.
Would she say lilac? Maybe lavender.
Here's my idea, she says, and I'm all ears:
No book titles, no prizes nobody has heard of.
No "debut" or "garnered" or "incomparable." No blurbs.
I'll ask each of you one simple question
and your quick-and-easy will be the whole shebang.
So… If you were a punctuation mark…

and I flinch. I see Barbara Walters on TV
ask Hepburn what kind of tree she was.
Trick question, I say to myself, overthinking.
Probably not a semi-colon is what comes out
first. I'm stalling, still in need of coffee.
Terri nods expectantly. Not an exclamation point
is my next attempt to keep truth in play
without letting it box me in. Her nod this time
gives a hint of miff. Not a comma either, I plod on,
and now Terri's annoyed, her brilliant ploy
foundering on a poet's refusal to follow directions.
Time's up, she snaps. Her felt-tip pen lands
on the pad with a flourishing curl and a jab
to put me down as question mark.

The Plural of Elvis is Elvi

Michael Salcman

Impersonators in Parkes Australia
and Las Vegas prefer
the late model who wore sweat
on his silk scarves and white jumpsuits,
his pompadour well-oiled
as black as burnt wood.

Much easier to ape Elvis in his cage
of sequins and rhinestones
than his sparkling youth
which flew out on Route 66
too soon, as we do;
each life just a half-written song.

The Yearbook of the Mind
Gabriella Brand

Be honest

The best kissing happened in high school and lasted
the length of a corridor,

skipping math class or glee club to slide onto

the back seat of a Chevy Malibu,

or, with difficulty, into the bucket seats of a borrowed

Corvette.

I'm talking about

the kisses that sloshed over onto the dashboard,
covered the windshield with

condensation so thick you could drink it
like raspberry seltzer.

The kisses that rooted around your mouth like a
pig looking for truffles.

The kisses that tasted of Oreos or Marlboros or
grilled cheese sandwiches from the school cafeteria.

The kisses that vacuum-packed your belly,

that sucked the air out of your lungs.

The kisses you

stashed between the pages of that yearbook we all
carry around in our heads.

Those kisses.

Amusement

Craig Cotter

I dropped a baby aspirin,
it landed on its side.

Jerry Kitchen and I used to drop coins
on my wood floors as boys

to see if we could get one to land on its side.
We did it once.

*

I finished shaving
2 days ago

and dropped the empty shaving gel can
in a wicker wastebasket

and it landed on its rounded head.
There was nothing else in the basket.

It's still standing upright.

*

Would you like to have this all tied together
in a new and interesting way?

I wouldn't mind
but nothing suggests itself.

Bernie rides the Ferris wheel
on the Santa Monica Pier tonight

with Vivienne.

All Together Now
Charles Finn

Leave the darkness to the crickets
They know what they're doing
Sawing away on bended knee
Carpenters of the night.

They build their songs
Little ditties of holy
Out of thin air, some cartilage
And the truth.

See how the evening gown of heaven
Sequined with stars waltzes itself
Across the ballroom of sky, how the moon
Cups its ear, rises to hear them.

The whole meadow turns out
Fireflies winking like lighters
Coyotes practicing their scales
An acapella of frogs joining in.

And so the question becomes
At what point do you not stand up
And applaud? At what point
Do you not fall to your knees

And weep? Saying *thank you, thank you*
To that eternally shy, famously invisible
Composer, standing before us all
Waving her silent baton.

What Is Similar
Melanie Perish

In Galena Creek, I saw
six trout scull in a line,
tread water between a small fall
upstream and an eddy
downstream.

What a consolation
to see the impulse, to pause
with others in concert,
to see some interludes
won't disappear.

My thoughts are
wet towels unbalanced in the washer.
When I ask, *Trout, are you a lesson
for a world?* they say,

*The day was hot;
the pool deep; not one of us
was hungry.*

Beyond the creek,
light dapples the steep bank
like nets.

Practice Run

Prartho Sereno

We get a few practice runs. One day,
for instance, as your plane lifts off your life
passes before you, the city below strewn
with spent days—at once devastating
and beautiful when spread out this way—
the potholed landscape of catastrophe & grace.

You'll feel like the bricklayer watching the storm
take down his wall, the conductor at the window of his
emptied train, the gardener at the fence after harvest.

You'll see the good bits were small but everywhere—
fine threads worked into a coarse weave. You'll see
what an immensity it is to walk & breathe & feel things
for which there are no words.

You'll wonder how you missed the tenderness
of the breezes in your leaves.

You'll wish you'd done almost everything
differently.   Then again
would you really change a thing?

Note From a Lost Pencil
Bill Simmons

You laid me here

With a bunch of pens

On the white phone clutch,

The one that holds the phone

That no one ever uses,

Surrounded by blank pads

Staring at the kitchen ceiling

With a sharp lead;

I'm ready to go—

Are you still looking for me?

Your bacon's burning.

New Groove
Brian C. Billings

The best way to learn your jazz is on the Net,
where no on-your-shoulder old lady makes you fret
about your freaky patterns and transitions.
You're free to lay down your conditions
any way you like. Funky and flip and no regret . . .

like a teenager loose in his dad's Corvette.
You're lost in the funhouse with every set
some solid player uploads for your ambitions.
Variety provides a wider sort of alphabet.

You pick up the measure of grit and sweat.
Style becomes your burning cigarette,
smoking off into a ceiling of petitions
to the stream of needle-dropped musicians.
Each riff you throw is a channeled *tête-à-tête*.
The best way to learn your jazz is on the Net.

Furoshiki
Ruth Holzer

(Japanese Wrapping Cloth)

If you need to carry a watermelon
through a summer afternoon,
or a book, or a bottle
of chilled wine
or a long, slender object,
a knife, perhaps,
to slice the watermelon
or to open the uncut pages of the book,

then this hand-dyed
silk cloth, indigo patterned
with red and gold koi,
when intricately folded,
will become a shape
fit for every purpose,
holding the contents
intact for your journey.

The Morning After
Gary Harrison

The morning after
  last night's hard freeze
    sunlight stirs the leaves
      on Bill and Meg's ash trees
    spurring a golden flurry
      gliding down, snow-like
        gathering in drifts
          over the walkway
            on the curb

In our own front yard
  four goldfinches
    flit among tongued leaves
      cling to tall sturdy stems
    and feed on dried-up seedheads
      where late bloomed brightly
        a grand gallery
          of Maximillian
            sunflowers

What a welcome joy
  this cold morning
    in mid-November
      the neighborhood awash
    in potent unmasked pigments
      shades of vermillion—
        amber, russet, rose—
          punctuating these long nights
            and short days

Driving By, I See Different Flesh in the Field

Robert Okaji

Sometimes there are chickens.
Occasionally a pig.
One time, a solitary baseball.
And goats, of course.
Horses in the distance.
A few dogs.
But no people.
Never. Not
once.

How I Read a Book of Poems

Ryan McCarty

I bend corners when I don't know
what to say. I make boxes
and rings around titles like my arms
holding something beautiful, pulling
it close to my mouth. Some lines
get all marked up just to say stop
flipping and remember moments
like these. Speak it out loud. Notice
how things end and begin.

Single words get circles,
like when I remember verbs
are what hump a heap down the road.
My own lines flap like litter along
the shoulder, wrecking the scenery
but, then again, folks can see I never
sat still with these songs. In my head,
my voice mixes all up with theirs.
We almost share the page.

Because

Craig Cotter

We were driving
unpopulated New Mexico

no people that is
going north

or some other direction
summer, blue sky

your poetry
                    taking us

when "Because" came on
from *Abbey Road*.

We were driving west
or some other direction

their voices dilating
New Mexico.

You sat beside me
as my CRX flew east

or some other direction
more perfect

than snipping basil
on the poached egg

Poem continues

because we weren't alone.

—for Diane Wakoski
—see Diane's great poem "Breakfast"

Pain and Pride

Thomas R. Smith

After Ken Burns' Country Music *Documentary on PBS*

Blurry black-and-white afterimage
of a boy or girl, of whatever color,
in poverty, deprivation, neglect,
possibly abuse. From such beginnings
the stories notably similar —
a provident mentor, desperate
persistence, finally a break. Moving
forward but always with that cargo
of damage, ending early or late
in catastrophe — the funeral performer
hardly able to sing for weeping
for the man who couldn't abide happiness,
the woman with the pure heartbreak voice
crashed in a plane when she was barely thirty.
Is it any mystery that the hard-
living should love this music?
From deep in the soul of the country,
the keening sounds of ghost generations,
their loneliness and grief threading
through the good times when community
stood up to division. And the musicians,
some of them foolish and some sublime,
and many a combination of the two, flashed
their moment of pain and pride, burned the wealth
of their beauty and youth on the stage
for us to hear and see, gave themselves
in the way of people who have nothing,

Poem continues

before they in turn entered that earth
of the grandparents who worked unheard,
unseen, dismissed by the fast world,
to be welcomed by the memory
that cherished them, memory of the forgotten
ones they'd kept alive in their songs.

Crossing Texas

Ellen Roberts Young

Curious as Odysseus in foreign waters,
we leave the curving interstate, drive
all day on a straight road, courthouse to
courthouse. County centers of order, units
small as territories of Hellenic kings,
link sprawling ranches. As earth changes
from desert to muck, Midland yellow
to Dallas black, measured miles declare
a human scale can tame the far horizon.

What holds dry west, damp east together,
a people whose pride is size, distance?
I'm not surprised this broad-shouldered state
hosts the space center, though shuttles
neither land nor lift from here. Would Homer,
whose hero ranged the length of his known
world, have had the hubris to tackle Texas?

Banker to Borrower
Joseph Hutchison

Lie down on the tracks,
Little Nell. No need to fret.
We'll free you in time.

Unceremonious
John Davis Jr.

What does one say, if anything,
while burying a small raccoon,
road-struck and rigored, found
in the front yard's grass before
a farmwork-full day free from rain?

I did not know your life —
brief, nocturnal — your rummagings
or foragings. Did you frequent
the creek a mile back in the woods?
Ascend the limbs of its cranny-barked oaks?

In this azalea bed, I cover
your grey and black form, hopeful
that soil is kind, that your quick end
gives rise to resplendent flowers
so bright they slow fast-passing cars.

My Final Facebook Post
Marjorie Power

A short enough statement to fit in large print
on one of their loud backgrounds:
I'm closing my account. Contact me at...

Emojis pop, weave past one another.
The face that cares, the face that weeps,
the original lifted blue thumb.

You've made a wise choice.
    This, from a woman who used to gush
    and spew exclamation marks.

I've enjoyed you here and will miss you a lot.
    Confirming that I must be confused
    as to where life lives.

Wise decision
    from someone in France who as far as I knew
    never looked at my page.

Sending love. Be well.
    The smallest sentences
    she has ever sent me.

Only best wishes!
    from the only
    man so far.

My email doesn't work. I hope we can stay in touch.
    Wouldn't she intend
    to get this fixed.

Remember, you've got a friend
in San Diego. I've moved here.
We could explore. Come see me.

Inventory, Central Park, May 20
David Meischen

Muscle-calved gondoliers pedal tourists in pedicabs
passing horse-drawn carriages from the Gilded Age.
Hum of electric scooters. Sibilance of bicycle tires on
smooth pavement. Leisurely promenade of baby
carriages, clustered talkers behind them—mothers,
fathers, nannies, nanas. Beneath vaulting elms, lilting
African tongues make music of the morning while
Spanish streams in all its iterations. Keen-edged
consonants of Slavic speakers break against the agile
glide of French. Runners sweep the curving drive in
spandex, sports bras, running shorts, sweats—lone T-
shirt among them in Texas orange with stark white
longhorn logo. A tiny frou-frou dog frisks to keep up,
bright pink bow among the curls on her forehead.
Beside the path—*tick-tick-tick-tick*—the little hammer
head on a rotating sprinkler taps out spurts of spray.

　　muffled pulse
　　of helicopter rotors
　　wingbeats in shade

Grasshoppers

Paul Willis

Last night, a warm fall night, a pair of grasshoppers
flew from the deck into our kitchen, attaching
themselves to the white tile on the wall.

One was a bright green, the other smaller,
a mottled brown—male and female
if grasshoppers are anything like birds.

Or could they have been of different species?
Sometimes that is what the sexes seem.
One by one, I captured them in a pale plastic

drinking glass, where they hopped and jittered
against my palm—and tossed them back
into the dark, where they had no color at all.

Glaucous
Sara Eddy

On the way to Albuquerque we saw a sign
that said ←COINS / (something)→ and we laughed
but now in Vermont I can't remember what something was.
So I go on Google Maps. I drop the little consenting
yellow person down on the highway and ask them
to look around with me. It's a fool's errand
(not the yellow they/them, they're just doing their job).

We pass ALOHA RV, and a Sheriff's car unable
to pull us over, a cyclist risking the state highway,
and all that dusty silvery grey-green sage.
There's a botanical word for that,
but I can't remember it, so I open a new tab.
I end up in an article about olive trees
written by an Italian botanist in 1993.

Then I'm in a list of botanical terms.
Aculeate, smaragdine, esquamulose
("not covered in scales or scale-like objects;
having a smooth skin or outer covering").
Then I ask P, who says "the botanical words
describe the physical characteristics that create the color."
It's too early in the day for that.

Finally Google just starts throwing words at me,
hoping one will stick: pluviosity, shalloon, tricenarian,
eudaemonic ("living life with a sense of direction").
Google is just trolling me now. I still haven't found
the word for that unearthly verdigris
that nearly made me sob for beauty
when we drove down from Denver.

So I flip back to my yellow friend and toodle down
the road a ways searching for the easy laugh, before I realize
we've gone the wrong way for miles and miles and miles.

Zuma
Craig Cotter

Four 16-year-old surfers
cross PCH from Zuma
to Trancas Market parking lot.

Mustang & 4-by-4.

Clean sand from their feet.

Drop swim trunks behind towels.

Talk about sex like we did at 16.

Say good-bye with gentle fist pumps.

Siempre,
Sarah Stern

Siempre, that's what the man at the corner
would say when he'd begin a soliloquy about his life.
Each day we heard a different version
of what I imagine were
his war memories intertwined
with the now we were all in.
But, *Siempre*, *Siempre* seemed to be his anchor
for something significant
that I wanted to know more about.
I connected it to his hands that moved
in the air, flitting, small birds.
This happened in Spain one summer
when I thought there was an order to things.

Author Bios

Brian C. Billings is a professor of English and drama at Texas A&M University-Texarkana, where he also serves as the editor-in-chief for *Aquila Review*. His poems have appeared in *Abandoned Mine*, *Ancient Paths*, *Argestes*, *The Bluebird Word*, *Confrontation*, *Evening Street Review*, and *The Woven Tale Press*.

Gabriella Brand's poetry, short stories, and Creative Non-Fiction have appeared in over fifty publications, including *Comstock Review*, *Room*, and *Aji*. She is a Pushcart Prize nominee. Her essays appear in *The Christian Science Monitor* and *The Globe and Mail*. Gabriella loves travel, languages, kayaking, hiking, and hanging out with children. She teaches languages and writing in the OLLI program at the University of Connecticut.

Don Colburn came to poetry late, in the midst of a newspaper career. A longtime reporter for *The Washington Post* and *The Oregonian*, he was a finalist for the Pulitzer Prize in feature writing. He has published five poetry collections, including four chapbooks; all five won or placed in national manuscript competitions. His latest, *Mortality, With Pronoun Shifts*, won the Cathy Smith Bowers chapbook award. His full-length book, *As If Gravity Were a Theory*, won the Cider Press Review Book Award. Other honors include the Discovery/*The Nation* Award, the Finishing Line Press Poetry Prize, and residencies at MacDowell and Yaddo. Colburn recently moved from Oregon to Maine.

Craig Cotter was born in 1960 in New York and has lived in California since 1986. His poems have appeared in hundreds of journals in the U.S., France, Italy, the Czech Republic, the U.K., Australia, Japan, New Zealand, Singapore, Canada, India, and Ireland. Books include *The Aroma of Toast*, *Chopstix Numbers*, and *After Lunch with Frank O'Hara*.

John Davis Jr. is the author of *The Places That Hold* (Eastover Press, 2021) and four other poetry collections. His work has appeared in *Nashville Review*, *The Common*, *The American Journal of Poetry*, and in many other venues internationally. He holds an MFA from University of Tampa and teaches English for Jesuit High School, also in Tampa. He is an eighth-generation Floridian.

Sara Eddy is the author of *Ordinary Fissures*, a full-length collection of poems released by Kelsay Books in May of 2024. She is also the author of two chapbooks of poetry, *Tell the Bees* (A3 Press, 2019) and *Full Mouth* (Finishing Line, 2020). She has published widely in print and online literary journals, including *Threepenny Review*, *South85*, *Raleigh Review*, and *Pink Panther*, among other venues. She is Assistant Director of the writing center at Smith College, in Northampton, Massachusetts, and lives in nearby Amherst with a teenager, a black cat, and a white dog.

Charles Finn is the former editor of the literary and fine art magazine *High Desert Journal*, author of the nonfiction collection *Wild Delicate Seconds: 29 Wildlife Encounters*, and author of the poetry in *On a Benediction of Wind: Poems and Photographs from the American West*, winner of the 2022 Montana Book Award. He is co-editor of the textbook/anthology *The Art of Revising Poetry: 21 U.S. Poets on their Drafts, Craft, and Process* as well as co-editor of the forthcoming anthology *We Are All God's Poems*. His second poetry collection, *The Folding Chair of Now*, will be out from Chatwin Press in 2025. He lives in Havre, MT, with his wife Joyce Mphande-Finn and their two cats Tija and Rilke.

Gary Harrison, a retired professor of English at the University of New Mexico, has published books and articles on nineteenth-century poetry, literature and ecology, and world literature. His recent poems have appeared in *A Wind Blows Through Us* and in *Abandoned Mine*. Since his retirement, Gary has focused his energies on writing poetry, hiking and backpacking, and composing songs. He is working on a collection of poems—"trailogues"—recording impressions of nature at home and in the deserts, canyons, and mountains of Arizona, Colorado, New Mexico, and Utah.

Ruth Holzer is the author of eight chapbooks, most recently *Living in Laconia* (Gyroscope Press) and *Among the Missing* (Kelsay Books). Her poems have appeared in *Blue Unicorn, Faultline, Slant, Poet Lore, Connecticut River Review,* and *Plainsongs,* among other journals and anthologies. She has received several Pushcart Prize nominations.

Joseph Hutchison, Colorado Poet Laureate (2014-2019), has published 20 collections, most recently *Under Sleep's New Moon; The World As Is: New & Selected Poems, 1972-2015;* and *Marked Men*. His poems have appeared widely in journals—most recently in *Pedestal, THINK Journal,* and *Poetry Salzburg Review*—and in numerous anthologies, including *New Poets of the American West* and *A Ritual to Read Together: Poems in Conversation with William Stafford.*

Ryan McCarty is a writer and teacher, living in Ypsilanti, MI. His poems have appeared recently in *Coal City Review, Blue Collar Review, Wasteland Review, Major 7th Magazine,* and *Rattle* (Poets Respond).

A Pushcart honoree, with a personal essay in *Pushcart Prize XLII,* **David Meischen** is the author of *Anyone's Son,* winner of the John A. Robertson Award for Best First Book of Poetry from the Texas Institute of Letters. *Nopalito, Texas: Stories* is new from the University of New Mexico Press. Co-founder and Managing Editor of Dos Gatos Press, David lives in Albuquerque, NM with his husband—also his co-publisher and co-editor—Scott Wiggerman.

Robert Okaji holds a BA in history, served without distinction in the U.S. Navy, toiled as a university administrator, and no longer owns a bookstore. His honors include the 2022 Slipstream Press Annual Chapbook Prize, the 2021 riverSedge Poetry Prize, the 2021 Etchings Press Poetry Chapbook Prize, and the 1968 Bar-K Ranch Goat-Catching Championship. He lives in Indiana with his wife, stepson, and cat, and his poetry has appeared in *Threepenny Review, Crannóg, Vox Populi, Evergreen Review, North Dakota Quarterly, Tipton Poetry Journal, The Night Heron Barks, Indianapolis Review,* and other venues.

Melanie Perish's work has appeared in *Sequestrum*, *Third Street Review, Sinister Wisdom, Calyx*, and other publications. Nevada Humanities featured her poems on the websites *Heart to Heart* and *Nevadan to Nevadan*. *Passions & Gratitudes* (Black Rock Press, 2011) and *The Fishing Poems* (chapbook, Meridian Press, 2017) are recent collections. *Foreign Voices, Native Tongues* (Single Wing Press, 2021) is her newest book.

Marjorie Power's newest full-length poetry collection is *Sufficient Emptiness* (Deerbrook Editions, 2021). A chapbook, *Refuses to Suffocate*, appeared from Blue Lyra Press in 2019. *Atlanta Review, Barrow Street, Mudfish, Southern Poetry Review, Dash, The RavensPerch*, and *Epoch* have taken her work recently.

Michael Salcman, poet, physician and art historian, was chairman of neurosurgery at the University of Maryland and president of the Contemporary Museum. Born in Pilsen, Czechoslovakia, he is a child of the Holocaust and a survivor of polio. Poems appear in *Alaska Quarterly Review, Barrow Street, Blue Unicorn, Harvard Review, Hopkins Review, Hudson Review, New Letters, Raritan*, and *Smartish Pace*. Books include *The Clock Made of Confetti* (nominated for The Poets' Prize), *The Enemy of Good is Better, Poetry in Medicine*, a best-selling anthology of classic and contemporary poems on doctors, patients, illness, and healing (Persea Books), *A Prague Spring* (winner, Sinclair Poetry Prize), and *Shades & Graces*, inaugural winner of The Daniel Hoffman Book Prize (2020). *Necessary Speech: New & Selected Poems* was published by Spuyten Duyvil in 2022, and *Crossing the Tape: New Poems* in 2024.

Prartho Sereno is the author of five poetry collections, most recently, *Starfall in the Temple* (Blue Light Press, September 2024). Poet Laureate Emerita of Marin County, CA, she taught poem-making to children in grades K through 12 as a California Poet in the Schools for over 21 years, and she currently teaches "The Poetic Pilgrimage: Poem-Making as Spiritual Practice" online.

Bill Simmons, B.A. in English/Philosophy from Fresno State, focus on reading and writing poetry. Mentors: Peter Everwine, C. G. Hanzlicek, and Philip Levine. Lived in Carroll, Iowa, for 20 years, read at local colleges, DMACC, and started a writing group with the instructors there and conducted a writing group at the local library. Now lives in Fresno, California, and is starting another poetry group.

Thomas R. Smith is a poet, essayist, editor, and teacher living in western Wisconsin. He is the author of ten volumes of poetry, most recently *Medicine Year* (Paris Morning Publications), and has edited several books as well, including *Airmail: The Letters of Robert Bly and Tomas Tranströmer* (Graywolf Press). His first prose work, *Poetry on the Side of Nature: Writing the Nature Poem as an Act of Survival* (Red Dragonfly Press), seeks to join imagination and activism in the nature poem.

Sarah Stern is the author of *We Have Been Lucky in the Midst of Misfortune, But Today is Different,* and *Another Word for Love.* Recipient of two Pushcart Prize nominations, Stern is also a six-time winner of the Bronx Council on the Arts' BRIO Award for Poetry.

Laura Winter lives in Portland, Oregon, and is the author of numerous collections of poetry, broadsides, and performance projects. Her poems have been translated into multiple languages, set to music, and performed as song cycles. When Winter performs with musicians, she uses the language of poetry as an instrument. Winter occasionally publishes *TAKE OUT*, a bag-a-zine featuring visual art, writing, and music.

Winter's US-Mexico borderlands collaboration with photographer Terri Warpinski, *Liminal Matter: Fences* and *Liminal Matter: Traces* is in numerous special collections such as Stanford University Library, Amherst College, and Yale University.

Paul Willis has published eight poetry collections, among the most recent of which is *Somewhere to Follow* (Slant Books, 2021). Individual poems have appeared in *Poetry*, *Ascent*, *Writer's Almanac*, and the *Best American Poetry* series. He is an emeritus professor of English at Westmont College in Santa Barbara, California.

Ellen Roberts Young's third chapbook with Finishing Line Press, *Transported*, came out in 2021. She has two full-length collections, *Made and Remade* (Wordtech, 2014) and *Lost in the Greenwood* (Atmosphere, 2020), as well as poems in numerous print and online journals. She has recently moved from New Mexico to California.

Special Thanks

We are grateful for Jeremy Warren of JWarren Designs who assisted with the cover layout.

Abundant thanks, too, to the many people who have chosen to support our mission financially. In addition to helping to fund our ads in *Poets & Writers* and keep our website up and running, etc., your contributions are incredibly encouraging.